DAVID FLUCI

IF COWS COULD FLY

Illustrated by the author

AUSTIN MACAULEY PUBLISHERS™

LONDON • CAMBRIDGE • NEW YORK • SHARJAH

A CIP catalogue record for this title is available from the British Library.

ISBN 9781398471986 (Paperback)
ISBN 9781398471993 (Hardback)
ISBN 9781398472013 (ePub e-book)
ISBN 9781398472006 (Audiobook)

www.austinmacauley.com

First Published 2022
Austin Macauley Publishers Ltd®
1 Canada Square
Canary Wharf
London
E14 5AA

DEDICATION

To
my forever darling Stine
and our wonderful children.

POEMS

Ali (the) Gator   6

André the Ostrich   8

Benjamin Barnacle   10

Bertie the Bunny   12

Bryan the Lion   14

Carruthers   16

Colin the Codfish   18

Swordfish Cyril   20

Dino (the) Saurus   22

Enzo the Elephant   24

George the Frog   26

Gerald the Giraffe   28

Hedgehog Hannah   30

Henry the Hog   32

Ishmael the Snail   34

Jimmy the Laughing Hyena   36

Armadillo Joe   38

Keith the Parrot   40

Lenny the Lizard   42

Lucy the Goat   44

Lukas the Lemming   46

Mark the Maggot   48

Neil the Eel   50

Ollie the Octopus   52

Percy Fitz Roberts   54

Rhino Pete   56

Philip the Fox   58

Priscilla   60

Quentin   62

Little Robin   64

Rocky the Horse   66

Seagull Stuart   68

Seahorses   70

Simon the Salmon   72

Stine the Starfish   74

Teddy   76

Toby the Toad   78

Ulf the Wolf   80

Vicky the squirrel   82

Wendy the Seaweed   84

X the balloon   86

The shoe   88

My Yellow Umbrella   90

If Cows Could Fly   92

A snail has no wings   94

The way you are   96

Swimming in line   98

Wash!   100

Colour   102

Numbers   104

ALI (THE) GATOR

Ali (the) Gator
Had toothache
And it was not
A comfortable sight

She was in great pain
In the morning
And I'm told
It was worse at night

When at last
She met her saviour
In the swamp
Deep down by the reeds

It was Percy the Pike
With a can-opener
That answered
To all her needs

He removed nine teeth
And then three more
It was they
That caused the hurting

The problem all gone
The pain soon stopped
In future
She'll floss for certain

ANDRÉ THE OSTRICH

There once was an ostrich
Called André
Strong legs, but weak eyes
Had he

He'd surely have had many children
But instead
He fell in love
With a tree

BENJAMIN BARNACLE

Benjamin Barnacle
Has a half million brothers
And each one of those
Has a half million others

So watch for your feet
If you walk with them bare
For it's not just Ben
But his brothers that are there!

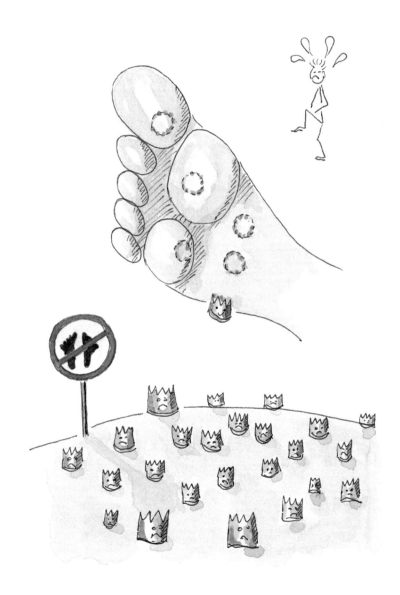

BERTIE THE BUNNY

Bertie the Bunny
Liked eating white honey
Which was strange for a rabbit
I agree

But Bertie the Bunny
Thought it was yummy
So he ate it each day
For tea

BRYAN THE LION

Bryan the lion
Looked scary it's true
With sharp teeth and claws
What else would he do?

But Bryan was old
And couldn't catch food
So his tummy would rumble
And the tourists would boo

Then Bryan the lion
Despite his long mane
Felt shy and embarrassed
And hated the shame

But once when poor Bryan
Got a thorn in his paw
He forgot his tummy
And the pain made him ROAR!

Now Bryan the lion
Still can't catch his food
But he's now found a way
To stop being booed

He finds the tourist
With largest lunch pack
Then he roars and they drop it
And then, he can snack!

CARRUTHERS

There once was a horse
Called Carruthers
Who couldn't run as fast
As the others

'Til his owner one day
Fed him curry not hay
Now he flies like a rocket
Above us

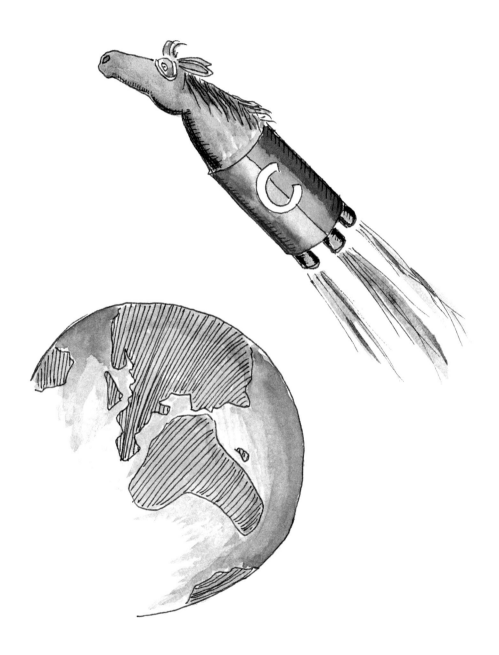

COLIN THE CODFISH

Colin the mighty Codfish
Lived down in the darkest deep
Colin the mighty Codfish
Found it hard to get to sleep

Colin the mighty Codfish
Was scared of the dark you see
So sadly our friend poor Colin
Stayed awake most nights 'til three

SWORDFISH CYRIL

Swordfish Cyril
Was sent home from school
Swordfish Cyril
Was banned from the pool

Swordfish Cyril
Was dangerous they said
Because young Cyril
Had a sword on his head

DINO (THE) SAURUS

Dino (the) Saurus
Played football with his friends
They were small with feathers
They were three brown hens

But what he liked best
Was to go for long walks
With his wife and his son
… and the hens, of course

ENZO THE ELEPHANT

Enzo the elephant
Liked racing fast cars
His favourite
Was Italian and red

He was good with the gears
And steered with his ears
And he was once
A champion it's said

GEORGE THE FROG

There once was a frog
Called George
Who lived at the bottom
Of a gorge

The cliffs were steep
The water was deep
So no-one ever met
Poor George

GERALD THE GIRAFFE

Gerald the giraffe
Had a very long throat
Where he tied the sail
When he sat in his boat

It blew from the East
And it raged from the West
So lucky for him
That he had a life vest

HEDGEHOG HANNAH

Hedgehog Hannah
Made a large banner
It read: "We're here
Watch out"

The reason was clear
As many came near
And hedgehogs as you know
Can't shout

HENRY THE HOG

Young Henry the hog
Had a tummy like a log
And his teeth were as sharp
As knives

But the rubbish he ate
Left his tummy in a state
So now he eats fruit
...And thrives

ISHMAEL THE SNAIL

Ishmael the snail
Didn't have any tail
But a house
Rolled up on top

In Summer he was sloooow
As his strength was low
But in Winter it was worse
It was STOP!

Ishmael the snail
Didn't move very fast
Because Ishmael
Only ate wet grass

But one day he tried oil
With garlic and pepper
He's still not fast
But the grass tastes better!

JIMMY THE LAUGHING HYENA

Jimmy the laughing hyena
Very skilled with a camera was he
He clicked far out on the prairie
And clicked high up in a tree

If you wonder about his name
I'll explain and then you'll see
It's that he never stopped laughing
After clicking a photo of me

ARMADILLO JOE

Armadillo Joe
Wore a woolly hat
It was knitted by his friend
A longhaired tabby cat

The reason that he wore it
If you really want to know
Is there was never any hair
On Armadillo Joe

KEITH THE PARROT

Keith the Parrot
Had long blue feathers
And a beak
That shone red in the sun

He was clever to speak
It's true to say
But he argued
Too much with his Mum

LENNY THE LIZARD

Lenny was a Lizard
Forked tongue
Long claws
And a tail

He bought
A laptop computer
Which he used
To read his mail

LUCY THE GOAT

Lucy the Goat
Went to sea in a boat
But the waves
They made her sick

So to make her feel better
She ordered good weather
And now all she does
Is hic

LUKAS THE LEMMING

Lukas the lemming
Sat on the cliff top
But Lukas the lemming
Refused to jump off

Because Lukas was happy
With the world and his life
And was deeply in love
With his beautiful wife

MARK THE MAGGOT

Mark the Maggot
Smelled of dead haddock
Did it worry his girl?
Not at all

Girl maggots have no noses
Don't even like roses
And to wriggle in rotten food
Is their ball

NEIL THE EEL

Neil the Eel
Raced his bike down the river
He could pedal very fast
But water made him shiver

By shivering and smiling
He was forced to drink
But each time he did
Poor Neil, would sink

OLLIE THE OCTOPUS

Ollie the Octopus
Had eight long legs
So to hang up his boots
He needed eight pegs

You see he had talent
And his boots were the key
At underwater football
He was champion of the sea

PERCY FITZ ROBERTS

His name was Percy Fitz Roberts
A feline from Bengaloo
He ate his toast with fire-tongs
And his milk he drank from a shoe

He read the *Times* whilst taking a bath
And brushed his hair with a fork
And in typical style as a kitten
He could sing before he could talk

RHINO PETE

Rhino Pete
Had EXTREMELY large feet
And a horn
Much longer than most

The secret of his strength
I could tell at great length
But in short
It was marmite on toast

PHILIP THE FOX

I have a hundred fishes
To wash my dishes
And a spider
To darn my socks

But who can I ask
To brush my shoes?
Of course –
Young Philip the Fox!

PRISCILLA

There once was a cow
Called Priscilla
Whose horns were so sharp
They could kill ya'

So her owner one day
Cut them away
And now all they do
Is tickle ya'

QUENTIN

There once was a chair
Called Quentin
Who although quite shy
Was able

So when he found a sweet bride
To stand by his side
Of course
It was Mabel, the table

LITTLE ROBIN

There was a little robin
He sat up in a tree
Close enough to hear him
But too high for me to see

He built a little nest
High up in that old tree
Although I could not see him
He sang his song for me

At last one day that robin
Came down from his old tree
He sat quite close upon a stone
And sang once more for me

ROCKY THE HORSE

Rocky the horse
Could run of course
But he often preferred
To sit

In a chair by the fire
In his evening attire
Where with needles and wool
He would knit

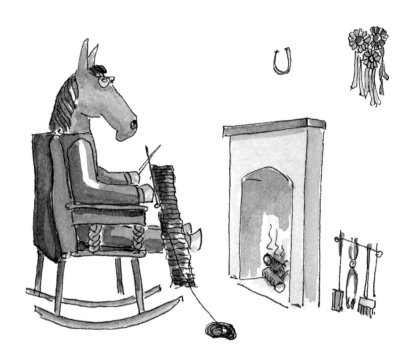

SEAGULL STUART

Seagull Stuart
Sat on a pole
Because his left foot
Was stuck in a hole

He pulled and he wriggled
As his friends they all giggled
Then "Aw!"
With a shout, he was out

SEAHORSES

A seahorse, of course
Never runs round a course
'Cause he has no legs
Just a tail

But he's happy at sea
For he values being free
We too could learn
From his tale

SIMON THE SALMON

Simon the Salmon
Had a bright pink vest
Simon the Salmon
Thought he was best

But sadly for Simon
This is such a short ballad
For only last week
He was eaten with salad

STINE THE STARFISH

Stine the Starfish
Had five pretty shoes
But alas to tie laces
She could not do

So bright as a button
And to not lose a shoe
Stine the Starfish
Instead, used glue

TEDDY

Teddy was not a watchdog
For her legs were far too short
But Teddy took care to remember
What her father had always taught

Don't worry if you're not massive
Or your coat is warn to tatters
It's not your outside appearance
But the size of your heart that matters

TOBY THE TOAD

Toby the Toad
Was bigger than his mother
Toby the Toad
Was stronger than his brother

In croaking and hopping
He was champion at school
But what he liked best
Was to pose by the pool

ULF THE WOLF

Ulf the Wolf
Lived alone in the woods
Where his friends
Came rarely to call

So to spice up his life
He learnt to dance
Now he meets them all
At the ball

VICKY THE SQUIRREL

Vicky the squirrel
Drank milk with her tea
From a tiny blue cup
Perched high in her tree

One day the wind blew
And the tree began to shake
She dropped her cup
But not her cake!

WENDY THE SEAWEED

Wendy the Seaweed
Liked washing her hair
But balsam
Was something she feared

For balsam plus salt
Makes weed go limp
And then
It looked more like a beard

X THE BALLOON

X is not
The Balloon here now
But the one that I
Had first

You see he had
To be replaced
Because one day
He BURST!

THE SHOE

Roses are red
Violets are blue
I have three feet
So I'm missing a shoe

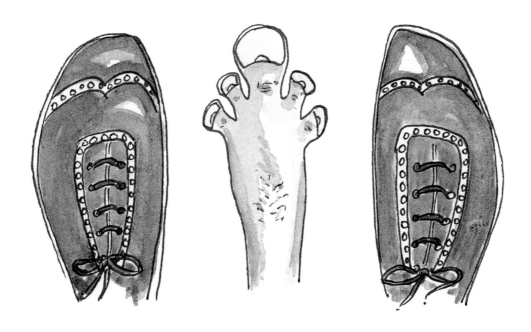

MY YELLOW UMBRELLA

I'm proud
Of my yellow Umbrella
He keeps me dry
When outside it's wet

He has no name
Doesn't even complain
When I stand him
Upon his head

IF COWS COULD FLY

Just think if a tree
Could live out at sea
With no earth or roots
Beneath it

And if cows could fly
High up in the sky
Then how'd we get milk
For breakfast?

A SNAIL HAS NO WINGS

A snail has no wings
A snail has no paws
No arms, no ears
No knees and no claws

Just a head at the front
With a shell up on top
And that's not easy
When learning to hop

THE WAY YOU ARE

Penguins don't fly
Yet they still have wings
And a bat has legs
But can't walk

So if dreams don't come true
Let it not worry you
´Cause you're perfect
The way you are

SWIMMING IN LINE

Five fat hippos, swimming in line
Until the 5th fat hippo
Decided it was time
To snort – "pththth" – and swim away

Four fat hippos, swimming in line
Until the 4th fat hippo
Decided it was time
To sneeze – "hæshew" – and swim away

Three fat hippos, swimming in line
Until the 3rd fat hippo
Decided it was time
To cough – "erump" – and swim away

Two fat hippos, swimming in line
Until the 2nd fat hippo
Decided it was time
To hic – "hic" – and swim away

One fat hippo, swimming all alone
Until that lonely fat hippo
Decided it was time
To turn – "swish" – and swim back home

WASH!

Wash, wash,
Scour and scrub
Dip the cloth
Into the tub

Wash, wash
Tidy and neat
Please remember
To wipe your feet

Wash, wash,
Clean and clear
Quite the best
It's been all year

At last, at last
I think we're all done
It wasn't so hard
In fact, it was fun!

COLOUR

My shoes are blue
My trousers are red
And I have a green hat
Upon my head

The flowers are yellow
The clouds are white
Without any colour
Would it always be night?

NUMBERS

One and Two
They lived in a shoe
And Three and Four
Had a house next door

Five and Six
Were perfect together
And Seven and Eight
Always happy but late

Then came nine
And at last her hero
Or was he the first?
I'm talking of Zero

ABOUT THE AUTHOR

David Fluck was born in Kent, England in 1964. He grew up as the fourth child of a country parson in Lincolnshire, and went on to join the Royal Navy. His last Naval appointment before retirement was as a NATO Staff Officer based in Norway.

David still lives in Oslo, and as a hobby, has designed several boardgames, written poetry and short stories, some serious and others less so, and is a keen watercolourist. However, what he likes best is to be with his wonderful family and dog Sarah, getting away from it all, to his small primitive cabin, up in the Norwegian mountains.